Weather Watch!

THE WEATHER
IN
AUTUMN

Miriam Moss

Wayland

Weather Watch!

Other titles in this series include:
The Weather in Spring
The Weather in Summer
The Weather in Winter

Cover pictures: Images of autumn – (Main picture) An apple tree ready for harvest. (top left) Rays of sunlight falling on autumnal leaves in the early morning. (centre) A dormouse preparing to sleep through the cold autumn and winter months. (bottom right) A carpet of red, brown and green leaves decorate the floor of a forest in autumn.

Contents page: An early morning mist covers bare trees in late autumn.

Editor: Deb Elliott
Designer: Malcolm Walker

Text is based on *Autumn Weather* in the *Seasonal Weather* series published in 1990.

First published in 1994 by
Wayland (Publishers) Ltd
61 Western Road, Hove
East Sussex, BN3 1 JD, England

© Copyright Wayland (Publishers) Ltd

British Library Cataloguing in Publication Data
Moss, Miriam
  Weather in Autumn. - (Weather Watch! Series)
  I. Title   II. Series
551.6

ISBN 0-7502-1184-9
Typeset by Kudos
Printed and bound by Casterman S.A., Belgium

CONTENTS

↓ *This map shows that we have three main kinds of weather on Earth. It is always very cold in the countries coloured blue. The tropical weather in the orange band is usually warm.*

The weather in temperate countries can be warm and cool at different times of the year. What colour are the temperate countries on the map?

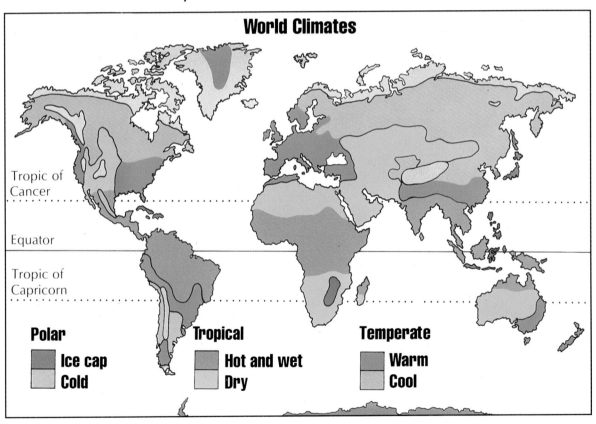

World Climates

Tropic of Cancer

Equator

Tropic of Capricorn

Polar
- Ice cap
- Cold

Tropical
- Hot and wet
- Dry

Temperate
- Warm
- Cool

↑ *These pictures show how the leaves on some kinds of trees change colour in autumn. The trees that don't change colour are called evergreen. Can you spot them in the pictures?* ➡

In temperate countries there are four clear changes in the weather each year. These changes are called seasons. The four seasons are autumn, spring, summer and winter.

THE SEASON OF AUTUMN

Did you know that Planet Earth tilts as it spins around the Sun? This tilt means that the Sun shines unevenly on Earth. When a country is tilted towards the Sun the weather is warm and it is summer. When the same country is tilted away from the Sun it is cooler and winter.

↓ *Autumn mists make the world outside look soft and mysterious.*

Did you know?

Autumn in the USA is called 'fall' - the time when the leaves fall off the trees.

↓ *This diagram shows that the way the Earth tilts towards or away from the Sun causes the different seasons.*

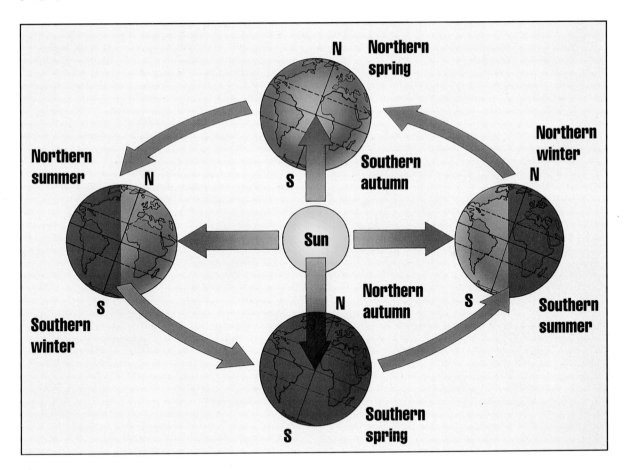

ALL CHANGE!

Autumn, lying between summer and winter, is a time of change. The long, warm summer days start to get cooler in autumn. The Sun sets earlier and the nights last longer.

↓ *The green leaves on the trees die in autumn and change to a firework display of blazing gold, copper and deep red.*

The nights grow colder in autumn. Soon the first frosts arrive. Everything is covered in a layer of ice crystals.

These frosty cabbages look as if they have been sprinkled with icing sugar! ➡

↓ *Crops, fruit and berries are harvested in autumn. It is a time of gathering in food - ready for the long, cold winter.*

9

AUTUMN STORMS

The wind is what we call air rushing from one place in the world to another. But what makes the wind blow? The answer is that air moves from one place to another as it heats up or cools down.

The air above the Equator (an invisible line across the middle of the Earth) is usually hot. The air over the Poles is cold. Warm air is lighter and rises up. Then cooler, heavier air rushes into the space left. This is when the wind blows!

↓ *The hot Sun shines straight on to the Equator which causes storms in autumn.*

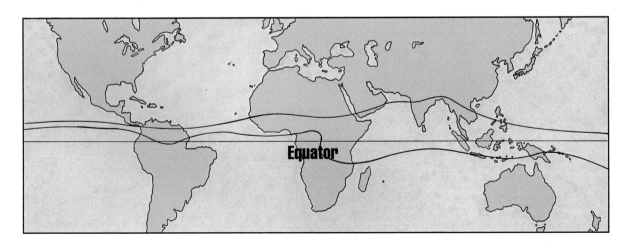

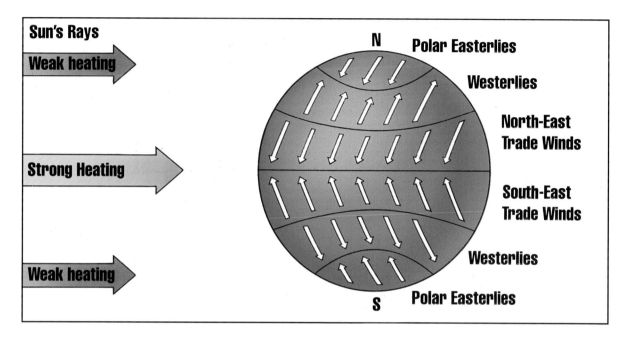

Sun's Rays
Weak heating
Strong Heating
Weak heating

N
Polar Easterlies
Westerlies
North-East Trade Winds
South-East Trade Winds
Westerlies
Polar Easterlies
S

↑ *The main winds on Earth have these special names.*

Rushing wind can be useful. It helps yachts to sail, washing to dry and kites to fly. ➡

The air around us has an invisible gas in it called water vapour. Water vapour is made from tiny droplets of water. We cannot see the droplets until they cool.

↑ *On autumn evenings, water vapour meets the cold ground. It cools down and turns into a thin mist or a thick fog.*

Frost outlines these spiky oak leaves in white. ➡

◀ Sometimes the weak autumn Sun is not strong enough to clear early morning mists.

WHAT ARE CLOUDS?

Clouds form when invisible water vapour in warm moist air rises up and cools. Then the water droplets collect together and we see white fluffy clouds in the sky.
Here are three ways in which clouds form.

1. Water vapour rises up from the warm sea or land into cooler air.

2. Warm moist air is forced up over a mountain and forms clouds in the cooler air above.

3. Clouds form whenever warm, moist air meets a band of colder air.

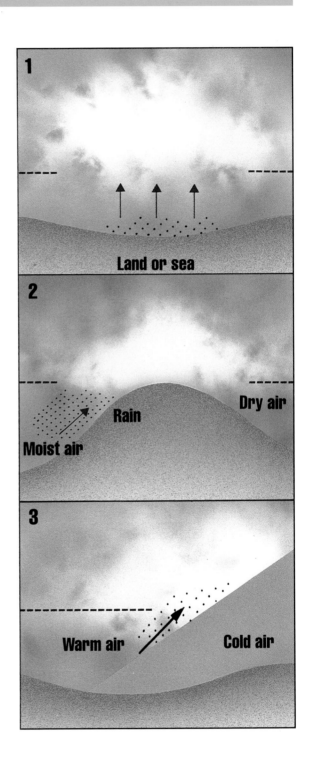

The wettest place in the world is the rainforest of the Hawaiian Islands on Mount Wai-ale-ale. It can rain here for 350 of the 365 days in the year!

↓ *Broken clouds can bring sudden downpours.*

↓ *This picture shows that sunlight, or white light, is really made up of seven different colours. They are called the colours of the spectrum. Light shining through the piece of triangular glass splits into the seven colours. They are red, orange, yellow, green, blue, indigo and violet - the colours of the rainbow!*

↑ *Millions of tiny water and dust particles in the air also split up sunlight. Blue light is scattered more than any other colour and this is why the sky looks blue.*

⬆ *The sky is not always blue. At sunrise or sunset, when the Sun is low in the sky, far more red light reaches our eyes from the other end of the spectrum. Then the sky and the clouds can look fiery red, bright orange or soft pink.*

WILD WINDS!

When the Sun burns down on to the sea at the Equator, huge thunderclouds form. The mounds of thundercloud pile up high into the sky. Sometimes groups of thunderclouds join together and grow into a fierce hurricane. In a hurricane, the winds roar at great speeds around a calm centre.

⬇ *Autumn storms rip up trees and cause a lot of damage.*

Storms are given different names in different parts of the world.
They are called hurricanes in North America, cyclones in the Indian Ocean, typhoons in the Pacific Ocean and willy-willies in Australia.

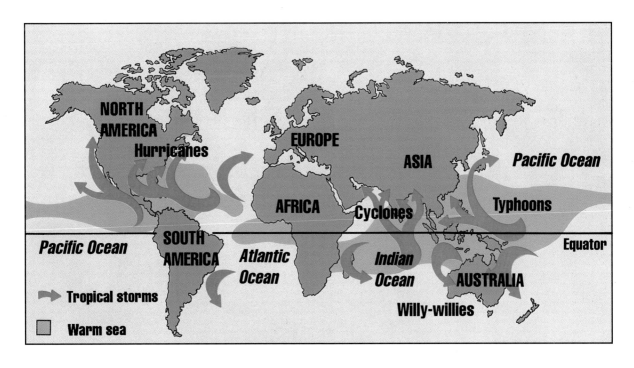

↑ *This map shows the places where tropical storms happen.*

The centre of a hurricane is called the 'eye' of the storm. Can you see the eye of the hurricane in this picture taken from space? ➡

Spacecraft, called satellites, are sent into space to send information back about the weather. They send down pictures of the Earth. Special cameras on board the satellites tell how much heat is given off by the land, the sea and the clouds. They send back colour photos showing the differences in heat. These help scientists to record the weather.

↑ *In this weather picture of Earth, the sand coloured land is a different temperature to the sea and the clouds.*

Satellites take a number of overlapping pictures as they circle the Earth. ➜

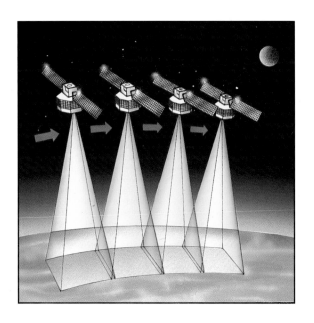

⬇ Satellites warn us about dangerous weather. The satellite below tracks powerful tropical storms in autumn. It also tracks the movement of gigantic floating icebergs and warns people at sea.

WATCHING THE WEATHER

It is difficult to guess what the weather will be like next week because the weather is always changing. All over the world scientists watch the weather. They collect information from ships, aircraft and satellites.
This information is fed into computers.

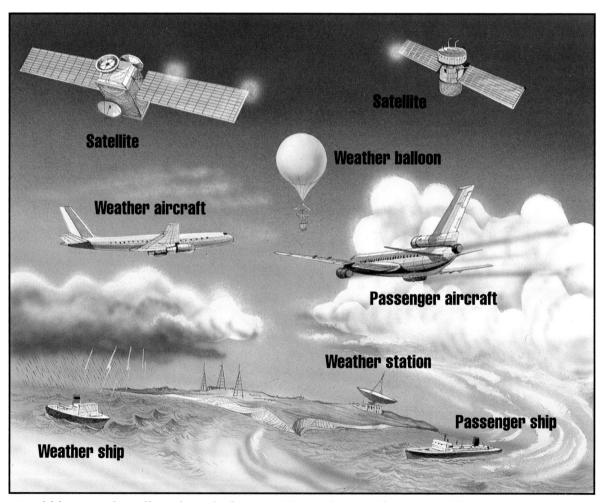

Satellite

Satellite

Weather balloon

Weather aircraft

Passenger aircraft

Weather station

Passenger ship

Weather ship

⬆ *Ways of collecting information about the weather.*

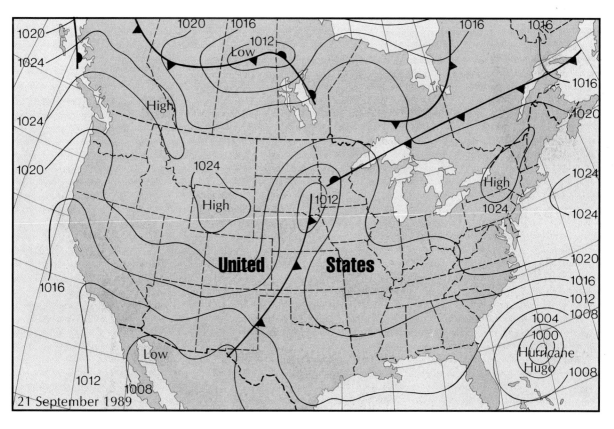

⬆ *The information collected from computers is made into weather maps like this one.*

The map above shows a hurricane, called Hugo, lying off the eastern coast of the USA. The map also shows areas of high and low air pressure. High air pressure means the air pressing down on Earth is cold and heavy. Low air pressure means the air is warmer and lighter. High and low air pressure bring different kinds of weather.

HEATING PLANET EARTH

The world's weather can be upset by volcanic eruptions. Changes in the temperature of the seas or changes in the size of the ice caps at the North and South Poles can also change the weather.

Many scientists believe that the weather on Earth is becoming warmer. If this is true, in time, some of the ice caps will melt. The added sea water will cause flooding to low lying countries.

Melting ice means more sea water. ➡

Gases spewed out by factories burning coal and oil trap the heat from the Sun. This makes the air much warmer, which changes our weather. ➡

⬆ *Sudden volcanic eruptions can change the world's weather.*

CRUEL WEATHER

Autumn is the time of the year when farmers gather in their crops so that there is enough to eat in winter.
But the weather can be very cruel. When the crops need rain, sometimes no rain comes and the crops die. When the crops need sunshine, there is a freezing frost instead which damages the plants. If crops don't grow then people and animals die of hunger.

↓ *A sheep farm in Australia after a long summer drought.*

↑   *A fierce hailstorm has destroyed this tea and coffee crop in Africa.*

This child has not had enough food. She is suffering from serious malnutrition. ➡

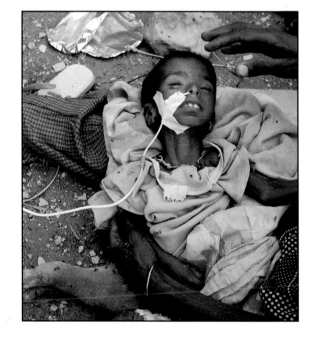

⬇ *We can measure the speed of the wind by using this scale.*

The Beaufort Scale		
Force **Description**		**Wind speed km/h**
0	Smoke rises straight up	0 - 1
1	Smoke drifts slowly	1 - 5
2	Feel wind on your face	6 - 11
3	Flags flutter	12 - 19
4 medium breeze	Wind blows loose paper	20 - 29
5	Wind makes small waves on pond	30 - 39
6	Telephone lines whistle	40 - 50
7 nearly a gale	Difficult to walk against the wind	51 - 61
8	Twigs break from trees	62 - 74
9	Large branches break off	75 - 87
10	Trees are uprooted	88 - 101
11	Some damage at sea and around the coast	102 - 117
12	Major damage on land and at sea	Over 118

An anemometer is the name given to anything that helps us measure how hard the wind is blowing.

The cup anemometer is used most often to measure wind speed. It has three or four cups which whizz round as the wind blows. A counter counts the number of turns. The speed of the wind is worked out from this. ➡

⬅ A line of washing is a kind of anemometer. We can tell how strongly the wind is blowing by how far the washing is being blown away from the ground.

anemometer Something that helps us to measure the speed of the wind.

drought A long period of dry weather when no rain falls.

flooding When water rises up and covers dry land.

frost A thin layer of tiny ice crystals which forms when water vapour in the air freezes on to very cold ground.

glacier A slow-moving mass of ice and snow.

hail Pieces of ice that sometimes form in high clouds.

iceberg A huge floating mountain of ice.

ice cap The huge area of frozen ice that lies at the North and South Poles.

malnutrition An illness which is caused by not having enough food to eat.

overlapping Lying with one edge over another.

rainforest A thick forest in the tropics where the weather is hot and wet.

satellite A spacecraft which circles high above the Earth. Some satellites send back information about the weather.

temperature An exact measure of how hot or cold something is.

volcanic erruption When liquid rock, steam, dust and hot gases burst out of a volcano.

Books to read

Explore the World of Weather by Robin Kerrod
  (Salamander, 1991)
Glaciers and Ice Caps by Martyn Bramwell
  (Franklin Watts, 1986)
Let's Celebrate Autumn by Rhoda Nottridge
  (Wayland, 1994)
Projects for Autumn by Joan Jones (Wayland, 1988)
Weather and Climate by Judy Langthorne and Gaye
  Conroy (Wayland, 1992)
Windy Weather by Jillian Powell (Wayland, 1992)

Picture acknowledgements
The publishers would like to thank the following for allowing their pictures to be reproduced in this book: Bruce Coleman Ltd cover, main picture (Hans Reinhard), 13 (bottom); Chris Fairclough Colour Library 9 (top); the Hutchison Library 18, 25 (top), 26; Frank Lane Picture Agency 5 (top), 13 (top); John Mason 19; Oxford Scientific Films 24, 29 (top); Photri 5 (bottom); Science Photo Library cover, bottom right (David Parker), 20 21; Tony Stone Worldwide cover, top left (Jerry Alexander), middle, inside cover, 6, 8, 9 (bottom), 12, 15, 16 (both), 17; Tropix Photo Library 27 (both); ZEFA 11, 25 (bottom), 29 (bottom). All illustrations by Hayward Art Group except page 22.

INDEX